ROSA PARKS

EQUAL RIGHTS LEADERS

Don McLeese

Rourke

Publishing LLC
Vero Beach, Florida 32964

PHOTO CREDITS:
All photos from the Library of Congress

Cover Photo: *Rosa Parks, 1964*

EDITOR: Frank Sloan

COVER DESIGN: Nicola Stratford

Library of Congress Cataloging-in-Publication Data

McLeese, Don.
  Rosa Parks / Don McLeese.
      v. cm. — (Equal rights leaders)
Includes bibliographical references (p.) and index.
Contents: Mother of civil rights — Teacher's daughter — Going to
school — Getting married — Joining the NAACP — Riding the bus —
We won't ride — Her heroism lives on.
  ISBN 1-58952-287-7
  1. Parks, Rosa, 1913—Juvenile literature. 2. African Americans--
Alabama—Montgomery—Biography—Juvenile literature. 3.Civil rights
workers—Alabama—Montgomery—Biography—Juvenile literature. 4.
Montgomery (Ala.)—Biography—Juvenile literature. 5.African
Americans—Civil rights—Alabama—Montgomery—History—
20thcentury—Juvenile literature. 6. Segregation in transportation—
Alabama—Montgomery—History—20th century—Juvenile literature. 7.
Montgomery (Ala.)—Race relations—Juvenile literature. [1. Parks, Rosa,
1913- 2. African Americans—Civil rights. 3. Civil rights workers. 4.
Segregation in transportation. 5. Montgomery(Ala.)—Race relations. 6.
African Americans—Biography. 7.Women—Biography.] I. Title.

F334.M753 P38555 2002
323'.092--dc21   2002002035

Printed in the USA

MP/W

TABLE OF CONTENTS

Mother of Civil Rights

Rosa Parks is famous as the "mother of the **civil rights** movement." She is a very brave woman. In 1955, Rosa was riding the bus in Montgomery, Alabama, when a bunch of white people got on. The driver told Rosa to give up her seat. She refused! "I was tired of giving in to white people," she later explained. This is the story of how Rosa changed history.

Rosa wouldn't give up her bus seat.

When Rosa was growing up, **African Americans** were not treated like white people. If a white person wanted a seat on a bus where an African American was sitting, the African American had to give up that seat. White people and black people were not allowed to sit together.

Rosa stood up for her beliefs.

Teacher's Daughter

Rosa was born on February 4, 1913, in Tuskegee, Alabama. Her mother was a teacher, and her father was a carpenter. They named their baby Rosa Louise McCauley. When she was two, she moved to her grandparents' farm in Alabama with her mother and younger brother.

Going to School

Rosa was a quiet girl who loved to read. When she went to the Montgomery School for Girls, one of her favorite classes was sewing. She helped pick cotton on her grandparents' farm, just outside the city of Montgomery, Alabama. After she graduated from high school, she went to Alabama State Teachers College.

Rosa was quiet and loved to read.

Getting Married

In 1932, Rosa married Raymond Parks, a barber. Her name became Rosa Parks. Rosa and Raymond never had any children.

At that time, black people in the South weren't allowed to go to the same schools, eat at the same restaurants, or stay at the same hotels as white people. Rosa and Raymond knew this was wrong.

Signs show how African-Americans were kept separate from whites.

Joining the NAACP

Rosa and Raymond wanted to change the laws that treated African Americans like they weren't as good as whites. They joined the National Association for the Advancement of **Colored** People, also known as the NAACP. In those days, African Americans were called "colored people," because they are a different color than white people.

A protest about segregated schools

Riding the Bus

On December 1, 1955, Rosa was taking the bus home from her work at a Montgomery store. White passengers got on the bus, and Rosa refused to give them her seat. The bus driver called the police, and Rosa was arrested for breaking the law. The judge found her guilty and said she had to pay a fine of ten dollars. Rosa knew the law was wrong.

Rosa was arrested.

We Won't Ride

After Rosa's arrest, African Americans said they wouldn't ride the bus unless they could sit wherever they wanted. They called this a **boycott**. Led by Dr. Martin Luther King, Jr., a minister and civil rights leader, the boycott lasted for more than a year. The bus company lost a lot of business. The Supreme Court said the law was unfair.

Dr. King with photo of civil rights workers who were killed

Her Heroism Lives On

Because she was brave and right, Rosa became a civil rights hero.

The Rosa Parks Freedom Award was named in her honor. In 1987, she started the Rosa and Raymond Parks Institute for Self-Development to help young people. She was given the country's Medal of Freedom by President Clinton in 1996.

*Rosa with Eleanor Roosevelt and
Mrs. H. C. Foster*

Important Dates to Remember

1913   Rosa McCauley born in Tuskegee,
        Alabama, on February 4
1932   Rosa marries Raymond Parks
1955   Rosa refuses to give up her seat on a
        Montgomery, Alabama, bus
1987   Founds the Rosa and Raymond Parks
        Institute for Self-Development
1996   Awarded the Medal of Freedom by
        President Bill Clinton

GLOSSARY

African Americans (aff RIH kun uh MARE ih kuns) — black people, Americans whose early relatives came from Africa

boycott (BOY kot) — refusing to buy something or pay to use a service as a protest

civil rights (SIV ul RYTS) — the equal rights of every citizen in the country

colored (CULL urd) — what African-Americans or black people were called through the early 1960s

INDEX

Further Reading

Kudlinski, Kathleen V. *Rosa Parks.* Simon & Schuster Children's, 2001.
Parks, Rosa. *I Am Rosa Parks.* Penguin Putnam Books for Young Readers, 1999.
Wilson, Camilla. *Rosa Parks: From the Back of the Bus to the Front of a Movement.*
   Scholastic, Inc., 2000.

Websites To Visit

http://www.girlpower.gov/girlarea/gpguests/RosaParks.htm
http://www.triadntr.net/~rdavis/parks.htm

About The Author

Don McLeese is an award-winning journalist whose work has appeared in many newspapers and magazines. He is a frequent contributor to the World Book Encyclopedia. He and his wife, Maria, have two daughters and live in West Des Moines, Iowa.